D1519632

Let's Be The Awake Ones

a month in poems

Meg Hutchinson

Published by LRH Music and Productions
Boston, MA USA

www.meghutchinson.com

Copyright © 2021 by Meg Hutchinson

First Edition Printing July 2021. Printed in the USA
ISBN 9781701378919

Cover photo and design by the author

Author photo by Stephan Hoglund

Preface

My mother has written a poem every morning for nearly twenty years. In April of 2012 she decided to lead a "poem a day challenge" for writers in the Berkshires of Western Massachusetts where I grew up. The inspiration quickly spread, and soon people across the country were joining in.

Each morning mom would send out a poetry assignment, a starting prompt for our poem of the day. We then had to craft something with the only time we had that morning, not trying to be perfect or polished, simply putting our pens to paper.

I released my first book of poems, "The Morning I Was Born" as a result of that month. In the years since, mom's annual April challenge has become international, with people as far away as Germany and even India writing with us.

These new poems are a result of another month of mom's inspiration. They mark early passage into mid-life with its sorrows and its mysteries and its grief and its questions and its soul-stirring cry.

If we're paying attention, it seems that mid-life arrives at our doorstep with the perfect combination of memory and pain and openness and restlessness and a longing for something to shift inside us. If we surrender to that longing, in good faith, it has the capacity to change us.

Since 2012, I've spent three years in Divinity school and one year in a large Boston hospital completing my residency as an interfaith hospital chaplain. Divinity school was gut-wrenching in the best way. I sat in the basement classrooms at Boston University School of Theology learning about the broken-heartedness I had never made space for.

I already knew depression well, that's been a dear old comrade during twenty-three years of living with bipolar illness. No, what I mean is that I finally was healthy enough to feel my childhood, and to trust my grief.

(Ah how I envied those steadfast Methodists some days, though, with their zeal for community lunch, with their capacity for secure attachment, with their sense of mission.)

It became vital to me in these years to know the dimensions of my own pain so that I would not bring it to the bedside of the dying people whom I accompanied. I wanted to bring the space that the pain cleared in me, not the pain itself to the bedside. I knew the only way to do this was to meet my own grief at my doorstep and to invite it in to teach me how to live.

I had noticed myself taking the spiritual bypass in recent years, wanting to cruise right past my own crap and show up for the pain of others. As noble and "selfless" as that sounds, it is not generous. It's like putting topsoil on the Goutweed tubers. They can stay hidden for a season, but they still have quiet plans to take over the garden. I have seen what happens when people in the helping professions bypass their own pain. It isn't good.

So that is what this lone Buddhist did for three years at the Methodist seminary. You'll notice in these poems that I also developed a keen lay-person's enthusiasm for cosmology, which had everything to do with needing some sort of existential ballast. I wrestled to know God, as a Buddhist among the theists, but somehow when I thought about string theory or cosmic microwave background radiation, or quantum entanglement, I felt the enormity of the Mystery wash over me.

So, I sat in the basement of that esteemed Boston University building learning about attachment theory and family systems and theology and trauma. Drawing up Genograms of my broken-hearted lineage, and feeling their weeping in my bones. Feeling the weeping of our country in these years of tenuous democracy. Feeling the weeping of the planet. This became a devastating and life-giving process. Maybe it was the Buddhist version of sitting Shiva.

We are made not just by the love, but by the pain of the ones who come before us. Before you can lift up your edge of the universal pain quilt, it seems to me you have to get right with your own little family patch, and with your very own thread.

I'm still working on it. But it's good honest work. I've been gathered up into the astonishingly beautiful fray.

- Boston, MA Feb 15th, 2020

***

I was preparing to release this collection right as the Covid-19 pandemic arrived in the Northeast. I had just started a new job as a palliative care hospital chaplain in Boston. Everything else came to a halt. Eighteen months later I have finally returned to set them free. May they be gentle companions in this time of grief and healing.

- July 31st, 2021

With gratitude for my beloved parents Janet and Jamie,
who showed me how poems can save us.

For Osa & Austin
joyful spirits, who walked beside me the whole way.

Contents

Consider the Narrow Places

All birth involves a narrow passage it seems
Through the straits of the birth canal
Through the narrow squeeze of mid-life

You have to die a little.
Small fish cast out of the womb
Old salmon pushing up the waterfalls to lay the eggs

That is middle age
Forcing up against the current
Tail flung like a wayward boom against the air.
We fight to get all the way back home again
Though we don't know why.

In order to be born into the second half of life
We must return to the narrowest places
        where the early pain happened
Where we became heroic and homeless for the first time
Gasping into the raw air
Pupils, once large in the dark of our sea chamber,
Shocked and shuttered into the light.

The soul flails against the Mystery like a ragged sail

We come groaning into mid-life like the shift of continents

Wondering if we are enough?

Wondering if there will be earthquakes

Who is this woman

Swimming vigil through the long nights

Who no longer fits into this small world,

       by accident, or is it by luck?

Even now, she is laboring upstream.

The Meaning of Life

Part 1

One afternoon I came across a dead snake

lying sprawled across the trail—

Its head crushed into the gravel.

I lifted it between two sticks

And set its graceless body in the tall grass.

Hours later, I found two boys with fishing rods.

They were about eight or nine years old

searching intensely there beside the lake.

"What did you lose?" I asked them.

"Our snake," they said.

"I found a snake. I put it in the tall grass. Why did you kill it?" I

asked.

"Oh, we didn't kill it,

we found it dead

so we tied it to some fishing line and we put it in the lake."

"Why the lake?" I asked.

"Well, because we thought we could catch a very large fish."

"Did you?" I asked.

"No, we caught nothing."

"Why do you want the snake?"

"We are just looking for the tracks of whatever took it."

"I am the whatever that took it. Would you like to see?" I asked.

They nodded.

I led them down the bank to a sheltered spot

where I had laid its body out.

Both boys grew silent.

When I looked up one was crying softly.

I knew he was the boy who had crushed the snake's head in

with a rock.

Part 2

What does this have to do with the meaning of life?

Oh I'm not sure,

I am just the writer.

It is still unclear… who is the snake, who are the boys, what is the lake?

But right now, all over this splendid earth,

there are people willing to do anything to get the biggest worm

to catch the biggest fish.

Okay, I lied. I am also both boys and the snake.

It is not too late yet

for us all to kneel down in the tall grass and weep.

Coyote

I would never have known

If my dog hadn't smelled him first.

Coyote, just a few yards back on the dark trail

Crouched so low I couldn't even see his silhouette

    slithering toward us.

Fumbling for my flashlight…

Light bursting onto the wildness of this creature

He stands to full height now,

so close I can see the hairs on his ears

Green marble eyes in the light beam

I try to yell, but realize I never learned how to

We always fought in letters in my family, back and forth,

Literate, bursting with metaphor,

      and completely out of touch with our anger.

"Make yourself tall the experts say!

Haze them, throw clumps of dirt if you have to

Be a bigger animal!"

No one could mistake me for tall

But I put my arms up anyway and flap them around

"Go home coyote! I am a humongous human!"

I yell in a sort of strained yodel,

Funny, the things that come out of one's mouth under pressure.

He does not seem to care. He holds his ground.

I've leashed the dog by now.

We begin our backwards mile to the car

"Don't run, don't turn away too long!" The experts say,

"It could trigger their prey drive."

Yesterday a man at the high school told me the coyotes

    brought down a full size buck

"Cornered it in the soccer field,

        must've been a pack of em" he said, eyes wide.

I think of this now, the pack

And our necks so much lower to the ground than a whitetail deer

"If attacked, cover your arteries with both hands

    just in case" they say.

I'm thinking of the anatomy app I bought last week

Magnificent 3D images of every artery and vein

You can peel back the muscle layer by layer

Strip away the cartilage

And peer deep into the chest cavity

    at the heart in its dark forest of lung.

Walking backwards is slow

I have a lot of time to think about those arteries now.

Each time I yell, coyote drops back a pace or two

Then closes in again,

He is all wolf and moon, all dark earth and secret dens.

There is a part of me that wants to be in contact

with something absolutely wild at the moment of my death.

There are so many unnatural ways to die these days

As a hospital chaplain I've seen enough

To wonder if I'd rather go out in the teeth of a coyote

than in the grip of a machine

When the time comes

But the time hasn't come yet.

***

Stephanie, the wild canid specialist, speaks to me patiently

on the phone the next day,

"He has no interest in you," she says

And I feel strangely disappointed.

"His pups will be born any day now" she says

"Somewhere back at the den the mother coyote is getting ready

Coyote needs to make a point. Your dog is on his land.

You could bring an umbrella or a baseball bat if it makes you feel

better."

"No, it really doesn't" I tell Stephanie.

"I can't even slap a mosquito."

She doesn't laugh. She's practical that way.

I can picture her back in middle school Life Sciences class,

eyes brimming with excitement behind her plastic goggles

Hand raised high above the Bunsen burners and the petri dishes

So she can get the first leopard frog,

in its moveable formaldehyde coffin for dissection.

That girl was my nemesis

I was never good at science.

My friend Hemangi writes to me from India,

"The coyote is thought of as a trickster, a joker, a shape-shifter,

A coyote sighting is generally a message to take a look within,

to not take life too seriously,

to lighten up, and to learn to laugh at ourselves

and even our mistakes.

Coyotes also remind us that anything we do to others will come

back to us—good or bad."

And so I wonder this morning,

What else has been following me

This whole time

That I cannot see yet?

And I think of that strange yodeling sound I made while yelling,

"I am a humongous human!"

And then I laugh

I laugh so hard I spit my coffee out.

It is you, Ego. Humongous Meg Human!

You have been following me around for forty years

Might be time to whack you with an umbrella.

Easter

For three days now

a crocus has been pushing up a small stone in my side yard

This morning when I took the dog out

I briefly considered lifting that pebble

But it's Easter, and that seemed, somehow, unnecessary.

I dreamed last night my older sister had cancer

and only two days to live,

We have not been close in years

And I'm still not sure why

In the dream I sob fiercely.

***

She cites Keats' "negative capability"

when I ask what happened to us

She says a great thinker is

"Capable of being in uncertainties, Mysteries, doubts,

without any irritable reaching after fact and reason."[1]

---

[1] John Keats in a letter to his brother 1817

I am not a great thinker,

I reach for her, even in my dreams.

I go back to the crocus…

I need to learn to live in Holy Saturday

To remain in the day before the miracle

To remain with the pebble on my head

Trusting that whatever force it is that brings all this green life

    bursting from the earth

Will work on me in due time.

I Am Here

It was my bedroom for nearly fourteen years

But I don't remember anything that happened there

Except the whooping cough,

In our little house by the edge of the swamp

With our falling down shed

blue shingles, and crooked badminton net out front

We didn't match the rest of that historic New England town.

I do remember the window, vividly

Covered all summer by a web of sweet peas,

Sometimes a view of Mrs. Stringham putting up her laundry

and pulling it back down again

Sometimes a bee or hummingbird

I had a lot of time to notice things.

I knew from a young age that my real home was out there

With the moss and the old quiet oaks

With the quince tree and the lilac and the skunk cabbage

With the muddy stream and the wild orchids

With the daily lamentation of the mourning doves:

They sounded like small earthen flutes

"I am here-here-here,

I am here-here-here" they sang to me from the white pines

Sweet and sad, sweet and sad, all mixed together.

The Appalachian trail passed by our backyard,

As mysterious to us as the haggard through-hikers

who drifted by on it

Sometimes so lost in their own thoughts

at this point in the journey

That they even forgot to wave to children.

Those strangers became familiar to me then

With their giant backpacks on,

their stooped shoulders and their refugee eyes,

People who don't quite fit in to the places they were born

Who make a home in their minds.

I became a turtle then too

Growing my shell thick across my back

Making my mind into a forest big enough

That one day,

I too could get up and walk away.

My sister sent me a quote this morning,

"Pain travels through families until someone is ready to feel it."[2]

Tonight I go back

I go back and I finally sit still there

I go back to the room in which I find out

My happy childhood wasn't so happy after all.

I am here-here-here

I am here-here-here …

---

[2] Stephi Wagner

I Knew a Dog

I knew a dog for thirteen years

Who lived in my house

Who woke me each morning with unstoppable joy for breakfast

Followed by impossible joy for walking

Concluded each day there wasn't ice on the lake

With a session of deep diving for white rocks

It began as a puppy when we lived by a clear stream

It was the white rocks she gathered

Deep down like a cormorant

Sometimes disappearing so long

I'd dive in after her

She was not like other dogs

You'd throw a ball or a stick

And she'd look up, "Is that the best you can do?"

But bend down for a rock at any point along the trail

And the banner of her tail would fly up,

her eyes gleam with attention.

***

It took me fifteen months to spread her ashes in the lake

I hiked out on the rocks to her favorite swimming hole
The wind kicked up at my back
Her ashes spun out from my hand like a great veil
They seemed to shimmer on the air
And then settled slowly down onto the rocky bed

I kneeled by the water, startled that they had not dissolved
Instead they streamed out there along the lake floor
An underwater milky way.

At night, when the moon reflects there on the lake
I imagine those tiny fragments of bone will light up
under the water

A small galaxy, that for thirteen years,
resembled a dog I love.

***

Weeks have gone by

But they have not moved

Despite the wind and days of waves washing up along the shore

The diving dog

Who she herself

Became so many tiny white stones resting on the rocky floor.

- for Osa

Poem a Child Might Write

I wonder if dying is like sleeping

But what if you have a scary dream?
Will there be a hallway you can tiptoe down
And a large bed where God can hold you?

The Joy Beyond Joy

1

This is how it looked the day you walked into my body. It was afternoon and the clothes were hanging on the line. The window was open and from our bed all I saw were trees moving in the light. When we came together, I flew out of the window and sat on the roof. You climbed up later with some cheese and bread. You spoke Gaelic to me then. The roof was thatched. There were chickens in the yard below. Your face smelled like hay. Don't ask me how I know this.

2

This is how it looked the day you walked out of my body. First you became a ball of red light in my heart. I began to feel the heat and my whole body grew luminous. A glass bottle filled only with your brightness. Just when I thought it would burn me, my heart became a dock and you stepped off of it onto the water. I did not know whether to follow. I yelled but all that came out was the sound "Ah!" I had become a bird. I was only a squiggle on the womb of the sky. You turned back once. Looking over your shoulder for me. Even the water was red. And behind your face I saw a mind that I had loved forever.

Theory of Everything

Neutrons and protons are made of smaller particles called quarks

Quarks go by some fascinating names like

up, down, charm, strange, bottom, and top

That sounds like the story of my life…

(But that is a different poem)

Now, beyond the quark

they are searching for "a theory of everything"

some say it all comes down to tiny strings

If an atom were the size of the observable universe

then these strings would only be the size of a tree

that's how small they are

I'll tell you how I got interested in all this

It was because I started to sit still

And got a glimpse of the universe beneath my ribs

I said to my heart "become a loom"

and I became the weaver

my bright strings woven in and out and in again

an endless cloth

I thought

if I sit here long enough …

***

Many people are busy probing space

with giant telescopes

or smashing particles together

in the Large Hadron Collider in Geneva near the speed of light

to see if they fly off into new dimensions

and that is all very important work

but it is the people in caves

high up in the Himalayas

who will tell you

"The only way to know it, is to be still."

Dark Matters

In the dark there was only space
and then the energy which had been pushed into a tiny point
exploded into a cosmos

In the dark the gases hung together in long strings by the
unspeakable pull of dark matter
forming so many hundred billion galaxies

In the dark it was impossible
but light happened

In the dark, most people choose not to contemplate
A universe which even now is expanding outward
at an ever-accelerating rate,
In the dark most people choose not to be aware
That billions of galaxies are ripping like waves through space
And crashing into each other in displays of ungraspable energy

In the dark most people choose not to consider
that even now our sun is reaching middle age
And will one day expand into a red giant,

scorching the earth before dying

just like all the other stars.

In the dark, most people, especially in mid-life

Choose not to believe that they will also die.

* * *

In the dark, everything is moved by gravity

That unseen substance

responsible for the death and birth of universes

In the dark two bodies bearing no tangible connection

Can even now be pulling strongly on one another

In the dark

Wherever you are

You are acting on my body

You are warping time and space

So that I roll around the valley of your sun.

Harvest

I have been wintering over for years

Suspended in the dark safe ground

where nothing can hurt me anymore

Is this the spring

Where your eager hands

Will pull me from the earth?

Heaven

The saddest kind of refugee is one
who doesn't remember where home is.
I'm not talking about the garden of Eden
I'm talking about when our consciousness devolved
to the point of separateness.

Look around you
If we do not know where we come from
There is no difference between a city and a camp
Both clusters of displaced persons

Of course, it all looks good down at the Public Gardens today
Little children on swan boats
Bridesmaids lining up like crocuses under the willows

But when they wake at 3 a.m.
Their loneliness amazes them
"Put me back in your womb!" the child wails

Dualism is brutal.

It's not the whole story.

After all,

If God made us up then we are still one with their mind

If the Big Bang exploded into a cosmos 13.8 billion years ago

Then we are still part of the stars

If evolution shaped us into human form

Then nested deep in our genes are all beings

And if all beings, as Buddhists believe,

have at one time been our mother,

Then even now, we are being infinitely held.

***

My teacher always says,

"Samsara and nirvana, two sides of the same coin"

Maybe heaven has been here all along.

On Being a Dog in a Library

Humans stay so busy and awake

If only they knew

How wonderful it is to lie on the floor

Just doing nothing.

Quantum Entanglement

"Imagine if you're in multiple places at the same time. What would that be like? How would your consciousness handle your body being delocalized in space?" - Aaron O'Connell [3]

In 2010, quantum physicist Aaron O'Connell

made the world's first quantum machine

Essentially a little shard of metal

That when placed alone

Demonstrated very clearly that it was both resonating

and being still simultaneously

One body with two distinct lives

This morning I woke up at noon

I made iced coffee and let the dog out

I sat alone on the porch steps watching him eat grass in the rain

I did not feel the rain

Because I was also with you

Tho I am not sure where

Einstein said that two particles who have interacted in the past

---

[3] Ted Talk June 2011

Can appear strongly correlated

when their various properties are later measured

Even if one travels far out into space

Maybe this is our story.

The Loss Game

I used to play a game
You will think it morbid unless you've also lost things

The game was this:
I'd think, if I lose my arms what will I do?
I will learn to hold a pencil in my mouth

If I lose both legs what will I do?
I will learn to walk on my hands

If I learn I have cancer what will I do?
I will run out to the fields and lie down in the grass
I will go to the lake and kneel down to smell the lichen
I will spend all afternoon in the hammock, loving this world.

***

What I never practiced for was a broken brain
Even words didn't make sense then
I wanted only death.

I could not leave, so I rode the stationary bike in that dilapidated psych unit. Switched on the old TV on the linoleum floor to a country music channel. I must've looked the wildest of all, riding that bike with the broken sideways seat in my private Tour de France, Dixie Chicks blaring "wide open spaces" out from that static.

During the smoke breaks in the courtyard
I took a basketball and practiced moving it between my hands
while the other patients watched

I was Alice in Wonderland
One day I even made the saddest woman laugh
My left hand had lost the language of my right
I was a fool out there
The ball sailing past my fingertips
Either too short or too long with every single pass

***

After seven weeks I began to want to live again
It came quietly
In tiny gasps

I became a sky-watcher

At first even breathing had to be done with a compass

This is the direction of the living,
Keep moving toward it.

One night on Baldwin Hill I noticed how the light
touched the tops of the grass
The next afternoon I saw a young man walking out of the barns
his hands filled with hay, his arms brown and strong
I longed for him
It was a longing to live again
And so I did.

***

I couldn't see it then
But even when I could not think
I played the loss game.

Train for it now,
If you can.

I Have Always Been Here

The original surround sound

Came in the form of bird song

Of air moving through the tops of the trees

Of the laughter of rivers

Tonight, when you come home from work

Before you turn on the screens

Take a moment

Throw open the upstairs window

And just lean your head out as far as you can

The moon will be there still and the stars

The April wind will move around your skin

Saying, "I have always been here

To hold your tired face in my thousand hands."

Music

Remember?

All we are is music!

With one beat the Universe exploded into the emptiness

And ever since then

Our infinitesimal strings

      have been singing.

Missing

At 4:30 a.m. a truck labors down my street

It stops at the intersection

A man whistles

A long plaintive whistle

Drives one block, stops, whistles again

And again two blocks away

This time I strain to hear the whistle fade

And then I realize ...

He too has lost his dog

Except somewhere tonight

his dog is alive out there on Spring Hill

Maybe eating someone's trash

Or following the trail of some dog scent

Or wagging down to the Mystic to muck amongst the reeds

My dog is not coming back.

But I know why that lonesome sound was so familiar

This is the whistling sound my heart has been making

every moment

In the 158,402 moments

Since I lost her.

Somewhere, even now

Whatever form her sweet mind has taken

If she has ears

I wonder if sometimes she hears the sound of me calling

from far away

And strains to hear my voice

And even if she has no ears

Somehow,

I think she might still be listening for me.

Time

"These are the old dog's ashes"

I said to the new dog.

He said, "Oh dear, will you turn me to dog dust too?"

I said, "Oh no sweet Austin, time will turn us both to dust!"

He said, "I don't know who Time is!"

I said, "Time is something people made up

so they could constantly run out of it."

He did not reply

And then we went to the reservoir together

And threw the ashes in

And lay there beside the lakes

forever.

April Song

The field is a page of music

And the families are the notes

I can hear it

From where I'm sitting

A bright song playing out across the green

It is springtime

The sun is angling down across the park

The women are quarter notes

Their pregnant bellies

Emerging boldly from their open coats

The children are grace notes

Racing through the grass

In so many glad clusters

The men

They seem to be the measures

that the others play between

Those lines dividing the beats

Into some sort of simple math

But the women and the children know
It is all chaos
And it is all music.

Thursday Night Chaplain Poems

I do not know you

But we shared your final day

I must tell you

Your breath was with my breath

On the train ride home

***

We are talking about basil and cucumbers

We are talking about cabbage and sweet peas

Now I'm blessing your stem cells

In their small clear bag in the nurse's hands.

Wow.

***

When I'm a patient I'm named Margaret

When I'm a chaplain I'm named Margaret

Every time I hear my name I remember I am both.

***

Mid-way through our noon-day chapel service

Part of the ceiling fell

Just a small part

On my friend's head

She is a chaplain too

There was dust and little chunks of concrete everywhere

Everyone was ok

After a moment we kept singing.

All the chaplains were singing.

Now I know what to do if a ceiling falls on my head.

Forty Years

Forty years ago this month, I was born

I chose the most beautiful month in New England

When the crab apples hang weeping with blossoms and when the

skunk cabbage comes marching along the shallow streams

And when the birds cannot even wait till sunrise

to begin their singing.

I have made it four decades in this form

Part luck, part grace

Part hard work

Part stubbornness that brings me to my kitchen cabinet each

night and lifts the lid of my pillbox and puts these small white

pebbles of staying alive onto my tongue.

Laundry

Fifteen years ago this month,

I wanted to die

Even more than I have loved this world. Which is saying a lot.

But I couldn't figure out

how my washing machine worked anymore

And I could not bear to die with dirty laundry!

Funny how shame nearly killed me

But ordinary shame, the thought of someone

picking up my dirty clothes

Kept me alive long enough to get to the hospital

To find out I had a mental illness.

What is broken in us, is sometimes broken just enough to save us.

Consciousness

For this brief moment

We can almost conceive of the infinite

And of our tiny place in it.

Throw away your books!

Run out your front door like a fool

None of what you need to know is in the Universities.

Refrigerator Magnet Poems

Teacher, laughing

searches our happy eyes

same joy lives inside all minds

*

Love dreams me lightly here

into your same fire body

this path is our home now

inside it we grow so free

*

Singing impossibly

I gave you the sky

our joy felt miraculous

behold, love is emptiness

*

Offering you the sea today

I now practice blessing this dark sky

gather me to sleep

our same dream forms eyes

I run laughing nowhere!

*

Oh heart teacher

gather enough water

in your many golden hands

become so lonely and beautiful

transcend craving,

grow absolutely free.

*

Run on home

our fire lives

beyond this wise mind

remember, I love you

in the amazing nowhere

*

I do remember where, amazing

your best eyes opened

we begin to dream

sit laughing man and woman

oh desire, whisper in now

impossible bodies singing

same emptiness songs

*

Let the sky hold me

choose HERE already

disappear you earthly love

inside I spark our miraculous joy!

Losing a Dog

"Your good dogs, some things that they hear
they don't really want you to know —
it's too grim or ethereal.

And sometimes when they look in the fire
they see time going on and someone alone,
but they don't say anything."

- William Stafford from "Choosing a Dog"[4]

Wake

After your death I sat beside you one whole night

Hand on your heart

Your heart stayed warm

The energy moved up my left arm and settled in my own

Breath

Though you'd been dead ten hours

A small sigh came through your mouth

The euthanasia was so fast, you never breathed out

It would have been strange to others

But I knelt down and pressed that last air free,

We never did need words

---

[4] From "The Way It Is" © Graywolf Press, 1998.

Bones

After the cremation

I ran my hands across your tiny bones

I never knew so much survived the fires

Weight

When I lifted you from the back of the car

And carried your large body to the warming stones

I realized it had been thirteen years

since I'd known how heavy you were –

This is a love story.

-for Osa

Where Does the Love Start?

Where does the love start?
Is it with what happens …
Or what doesn't happen?

One fleeting love story
and a wake of broken days
The pursuit of happiness leads mostly to betrayal

Hah! As if your old sadness won't find you at your new lover's house.

Here in the desire realm,
Staying is the crucible.

Desire will work on you if you ask it to. Be still in the flames.

Even now, we are radiant in the light of those smelting fires.

Alive

On Sunday it was pouring rain but I took the dog out anyway.
I was anxious. Sometimes the brain still tries to knot itself this
time of year. Sometimes the cold water cools my forehead just
enough. We headed down to Columbus Park.

I saw her instantly, the way you never stop seeing suicide when
your brain has longed for it. I saw her grey car and the hose
and the purple tape she used to fix it to her window so perfectly,
and the idling sound it made, strange and muffled.

She did not think anyone would walk in such a rain.
And I knocked on her dark window, thinking today is the day I
find a dead person. But she was not dead.
We spoke. I couldn't think of anything except the truth.

"Please don't die, I said. I almost did once. I do not want you to
die." It wasn't any of the right things I've learned about suicide
prevention. It wasn't subtle or trained. It was the plain truth, and
the pouring rain, and her eyes so dark and focused. I was looking
in a mirror.

This was a girl as stubborn and as hungry for death as I had been once. Look how perfectly she attached that hose and taped it up so carefully into the window. She clutched it while we spoke, like the reins of a horse. I could not believe my admiration.

She told me she was fine, "Just doing a little test to see if my car will pass emissions." It took me a minute to call for help. It took me back to a time when nothing made sense. I knew how deeply she dreamed of nothingness. How many nights she had lain awake. How she had waited for the pouring rain when no one would find her down here on this dead end road.

She turned the car abruptly and sped away.

When I called the police again, hours later, they said they had found her. She was living.
"That's all I can tell you" the officer said.

I wept in my kitchen then
in a way I never have.
Thank God for one more night when this girl with the dark eyes who I know from deep inside me, is still alive.

***

I will think of you each May, when the rains come

When the little white flowers of the Autumn Olive line the

roadsides with that smell worth staying on earth for

And I will wonder if you did?

I will wonder if you could bear to stay alive

After the night I found you.

I want to tell you, it gets better.

But that's not a promise any of us can make for one another.

Borrowed Things

Some days when I am not sure who I am

I stand before the mirror and practice being made

of borrowed things

My mother's father's dark eyebrows

My mother's mother's round cheeks

My father's mother's nose

And this glint of mischief right behind my eyes?

That is old Hutch,

Cowboy, horse wrangler, word man

This freckled skin my father brought me

from the North of Ireland

And when they formed my spine

They placed me in the crooked mold

They placed my mother in

So you see, I've been entrusted with this meeting place of beings

This meeting place of pain.

This intricate web of love-making,

making and making its way down through the centuries

Carried over from the old country

And below this skin I am just a conversation between elements

Earth, water, fire, air

Is there anything you could call a self in there?

Beyond that

They say we are really just the dust of stars

What tenderness, to learn

This pain body isn't ours.

Starry Night

It was painted thirteen months before he shot himself

Near the mental asylum of Saint-Rémy

He would have been exactly my age then

The painting is proof that he knew in 1889

The savage nature of a universe that science later would describe

A universe started with a cosmic shotgun

Galaxies colliding endlessly

A space rampant with dark matter,

shaped by giant waves of sound

Beneath that churning sky

Van Gogh painted a lone church steeple

Man's search for meaning

So impossibly small under that ocean

This afternoon I will go out to my favorite lake with the dog

My true asylum

Brain steadied by the drug

Glad not to be a genius

Gladder still to be alive.

Expanding

Since the universe is expanding at ever greater speeds

Into the vastness of space

Shouldn't our hearts be also?

180 Second Hope Statement

(At the end of my Theology & Trauma class we were asked to write a three minute personal statement about hope.)

There is a quote by a great Buddhist master,

"Because the thought of abandonment and achievement is not possessed, the absence of the harm of hope and fear is amazing."[5]

I had never thought of hope as something that could cause harm!

But the more I sat with those words

the more true they started to feel.

***

Hope can close the story in

Hope can interfere with grief or sadness when applied too soon

We use hope to tidy up a diagnosis, we use hope to turn away

from our own mortality

We hope that good things won't ever change

We hope for something that hasn't happened yet

But in the midst of our hoping for something else… often the present moment slips quietly right through the center of our lives unnoticed, uninhabited

This is how hope can haunt us.

---

[5] Jetsun Rinpoche Dragpa Gyaltsen from the "Great Song of Experience"

***

So I'm learning to think of hope in a new way

What does hope feel like if we get beyond "the thought of

abandonment and achievement?"

Hope is starting to feel more like a resonance, a frequency.

****

Music and mental illness are woven together

through the generations of my family

I've inherited my grandmother's guitar and my uncle's guitar

I'm left with the question of how to work with these genes?

How to work with the suffering of my ancestors in a way that can
do some healing?

****

People say that the longer you play an instrument

the more resonant the tone becomes. It "opens up" over time

Year after year the music is slowly changing the very structure of
the wood

If this wood can change, then my body can change also

I feel that resonance when I'm singing and when I'm sitting still

I get a glimpse of a space beyond both hope and fear, beyond achievement or abandonment.

****

Maybe there is such a thing as being "empty" with hope?

Without space, the bell can't ring

As my teacher always says, "where there is emptiness, everything is possible."

It's a summer afternoon. I'm twelve years old sitting in the front seat. My sister Tess is eight. Mom is driving us to our favorite swimming hole near Seekonk Crossroad. We're waiting to make a left turn.

Suddenly we hear the terrible squeal of brakes from an oncoming car.

This is what I remember. Mom looking in the rearview mirror. The way her face falls ashen in that split second. She can see a car flying up behind us, too fast to stop. Her knuckles go white on the gear shift and she says calmly, "Ok, this is it."

What happens next astonishes us all. The car accelerates instead. His only option is to get past us seconds faster than the oncoming car.

He does. He makes it. And vanishes around the next bend in a whirl of dust.

Mom looks over. I stare back at my little sister. Her hair all summery tangles. The sweet dark brown eyes enormous. We are still alive. Mom is shaking now.

All the other cars pull over. The oncoming car is filled with people coming home from a funeral. We stand there at the crossroad hugging these strangers under the tall pine trees. None of us quite sure yet if we have survived.

***

It was several hours before the rush of adrenaline left the soles of my feet. What I remember is how staggeringly beautiful the river seemed that afternoon. I remember the freckles on my friend Jessie's face. The cool damp body of the frog I caught and held in my palm and then so gently returned to his deep green pool of water. Just as whatever Gods who had been holding us, had so gently set us back into the river of our lives that afternoon.

***

Whenever I begin to take anything for granted I go back to that day. To my mom's words, "Ok, this is it." To the simplicity and to the wonder of being alive.

Wherever you are right now, find the nearest door

and walk through it

Let's go down to the river

Be gathered up into the grace of it all

Let's be the awake ones.

Acknowledgements

Thank you to all the forests that have given me refuge. To my sister Tess. To family and beloved friends. To WP. To Boston University School of Theology, BWH, and my teachers there. To Osa and Austin. To grief. To music. To my teacher and spiritual community at the Sakya Center. To unrequited love. To my ancestors. To chaplains everywhere. To death, for teaching me how to be here.

www.meghutchinson.com

"Losing a Dog" first published in *North Dakota Quarterly* May 2014

"The Meaning of Life" first published in *Anchor Magazine* Issue 5 June 2016

Made in the USA
Middletown, DE
15 August 2021